T0400517

# HOW DO YOU BUILD?

# How Do You Build an Airplane?

by Bryan Langdo

2

BELLWETHER MEDIA • MINNEAPOLIS, MN

**Blastoff! Readers** are carefully developed by literacy experts to build reading stamina and move students toward fluency by combining standards-based content with developmentally appropriate text.

**Level 1** provides the most support through repetition of high-frequency words, light text, predictable sentence patterns, and strong visual support.

**Level 2** offers early readers a bit more challenge through varied sentences, increased text load, and text-supportive special features.

**Level 3** advances early-fluent readers toward fluency through increased text load, less reliance on photos, advancing concepts, longer sentences, and more complex special features.

★ **Blastoff! Universe**

**Reading Level**

**Grade K**

**Grades 1–3**

**Grade 4**

This edition first published in 2026 by Bellwether Media, Inc.

No part of this publication may be reproduced in whole or in part without written permission of the publisher. For information regarding permission, write to Bellwether Media, Inc., Attention: Permissions Department, 3500 American Blvd W, Suite 150, Bloomington, MN 55431.

Library of Congress Cataloging-in-Publication Data

LC record for How Do You Build an Airplane? available at: https://lccn.loc.gov/2025010706

Editor: Rachael Barnes     Book Designer: Josh Brink

Printed in the United States of America, North Mankato, MN.

# Table of Contents

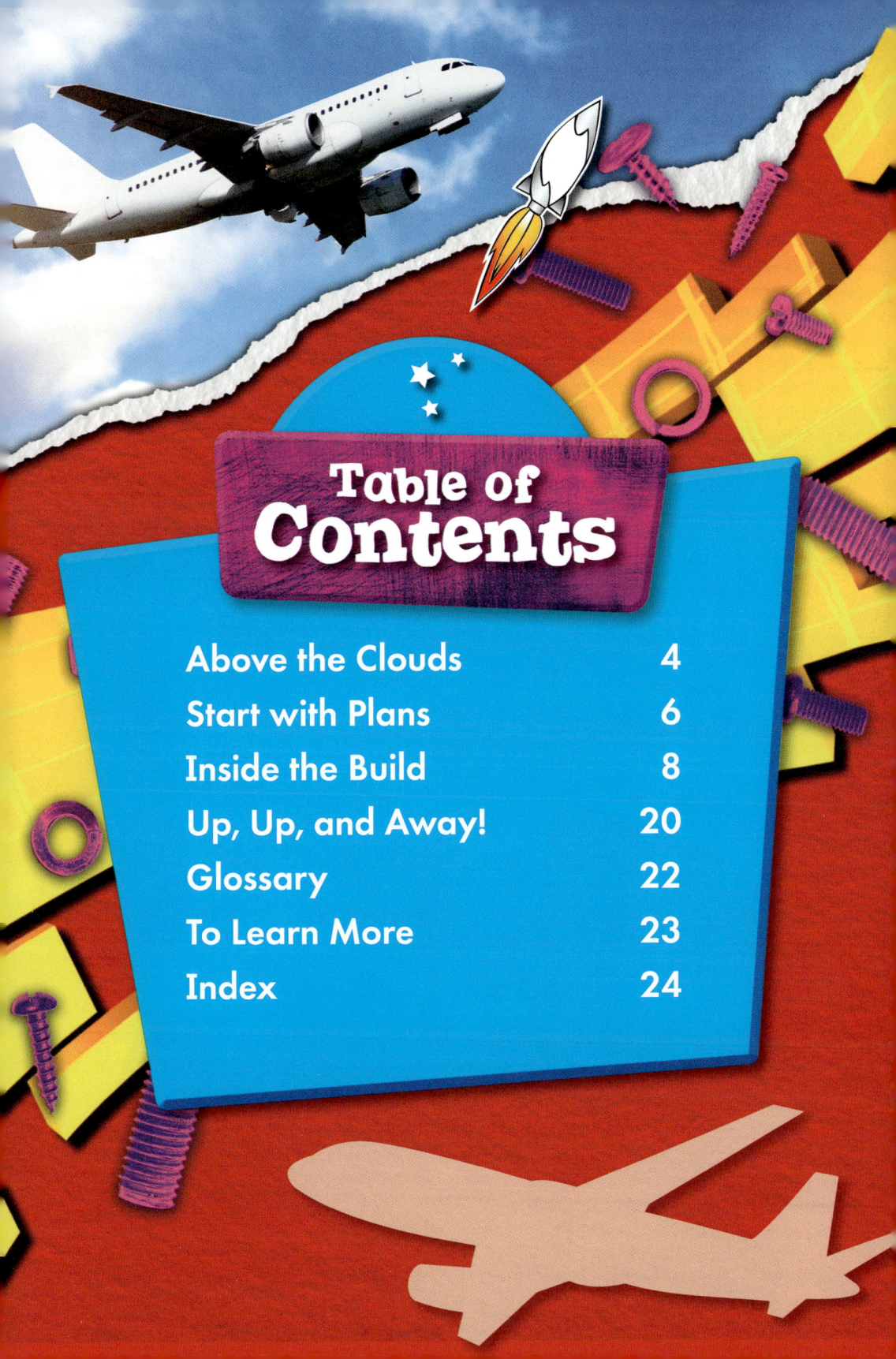

# Above the Clouds

A child looks out a window. She sees clouds down below.

She is flying in an airplane!

# Start with Plans

wind tunnel

model

**Aeronautical engineers** create plans and **models** for airplanes. They test models in **wind tunnels**.

6

Then a pilot takes a **prototype** on a test flight!

prototype

7

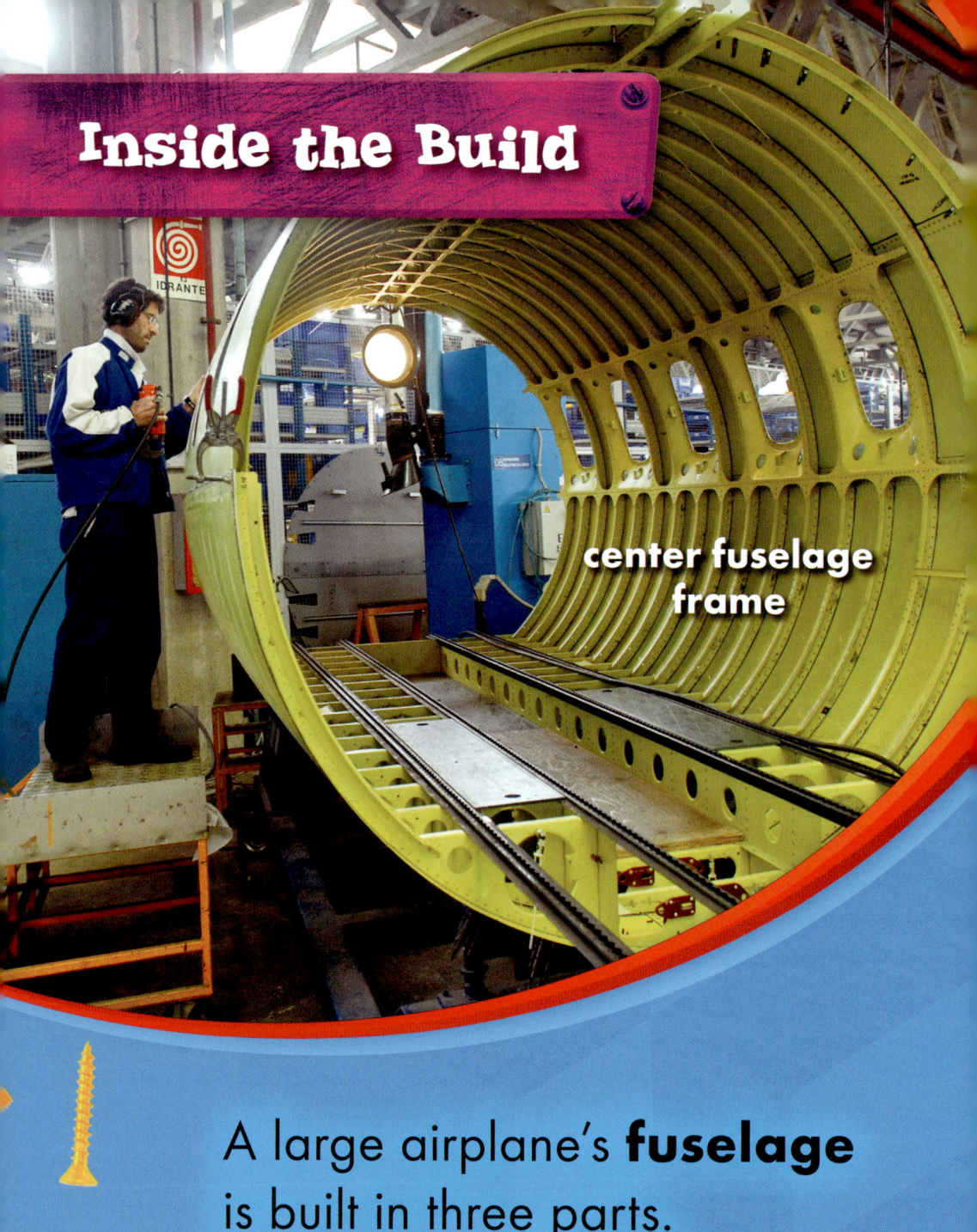

# Inside the Build

center fuselage frame

A large airplane's **fuselage** is built in three parts. The nose, center, and tail all start with frames.

8

The frames are covered in metal or **carbon fiber**.

## What Do You Need?

carbon fiber

rivets

glue

aluminum

rubber

9

Workers **insulate** the three fuselage parts. They put in windows.

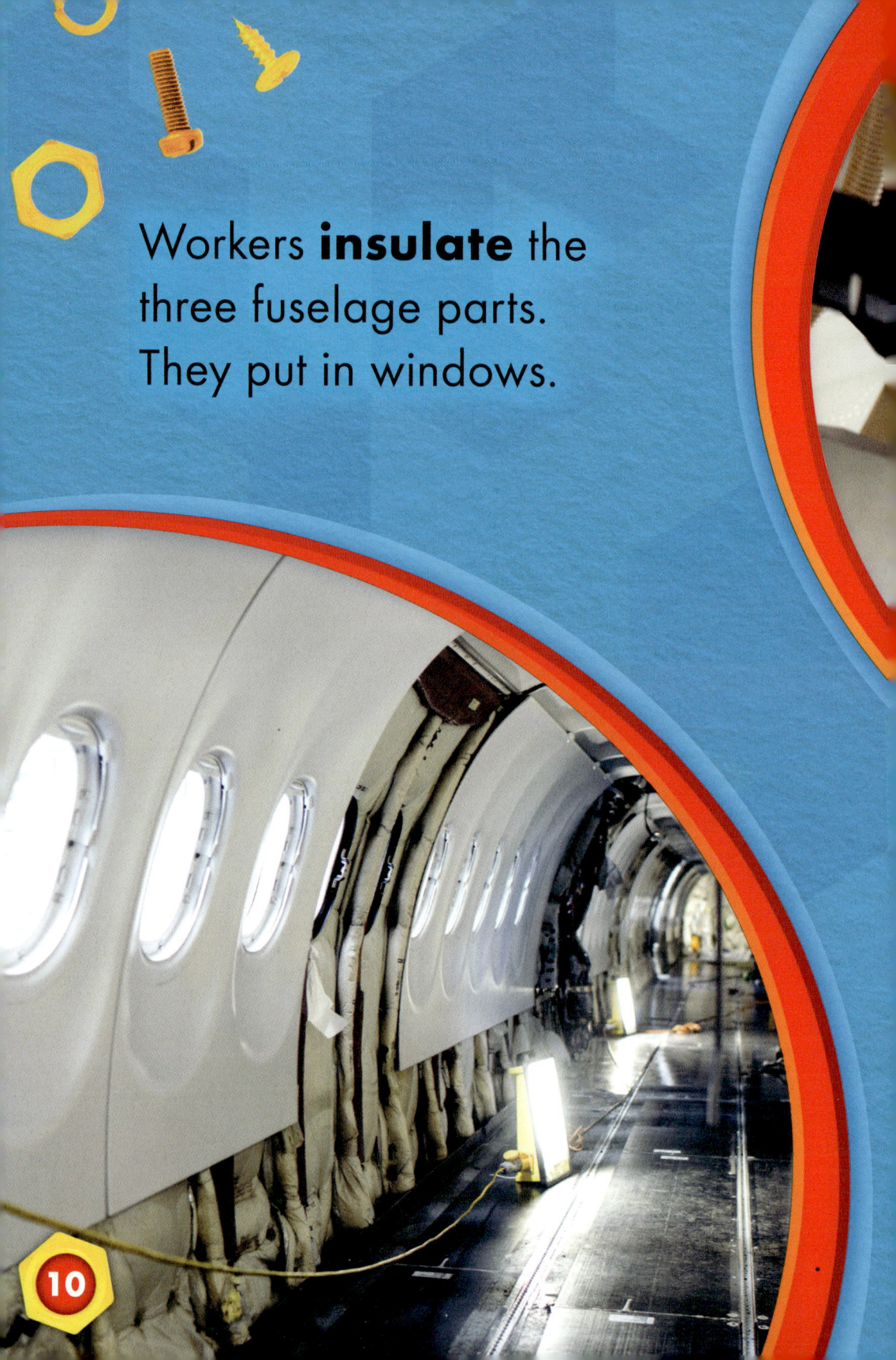

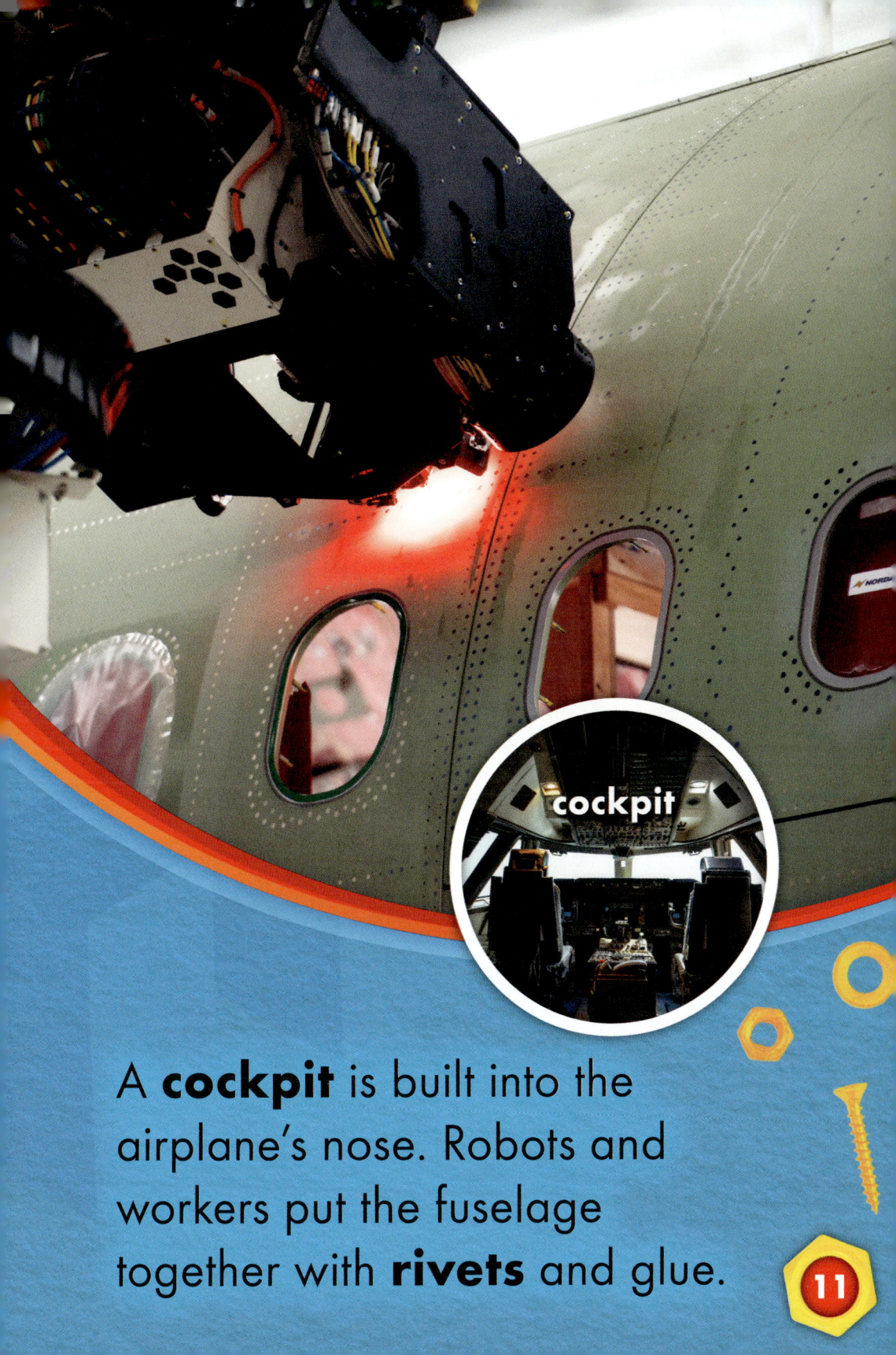

cockpit

A **cockpit** is built into the airplane's nose. Robots and workers put the fuselage together with **rivets** and glue.

11

aluminum
frame

The airplane's wings start
with **aluminum** frames.
Panels cover these frames.

12

Wires will connect the wings' moving parts to a computer.

cabin

cockpit

engines

wings

landing gear

13

Workers build the cabin inside the fuselage. They lay floors and add seats.

Storage bins go above the seats. Workers add lights, too.

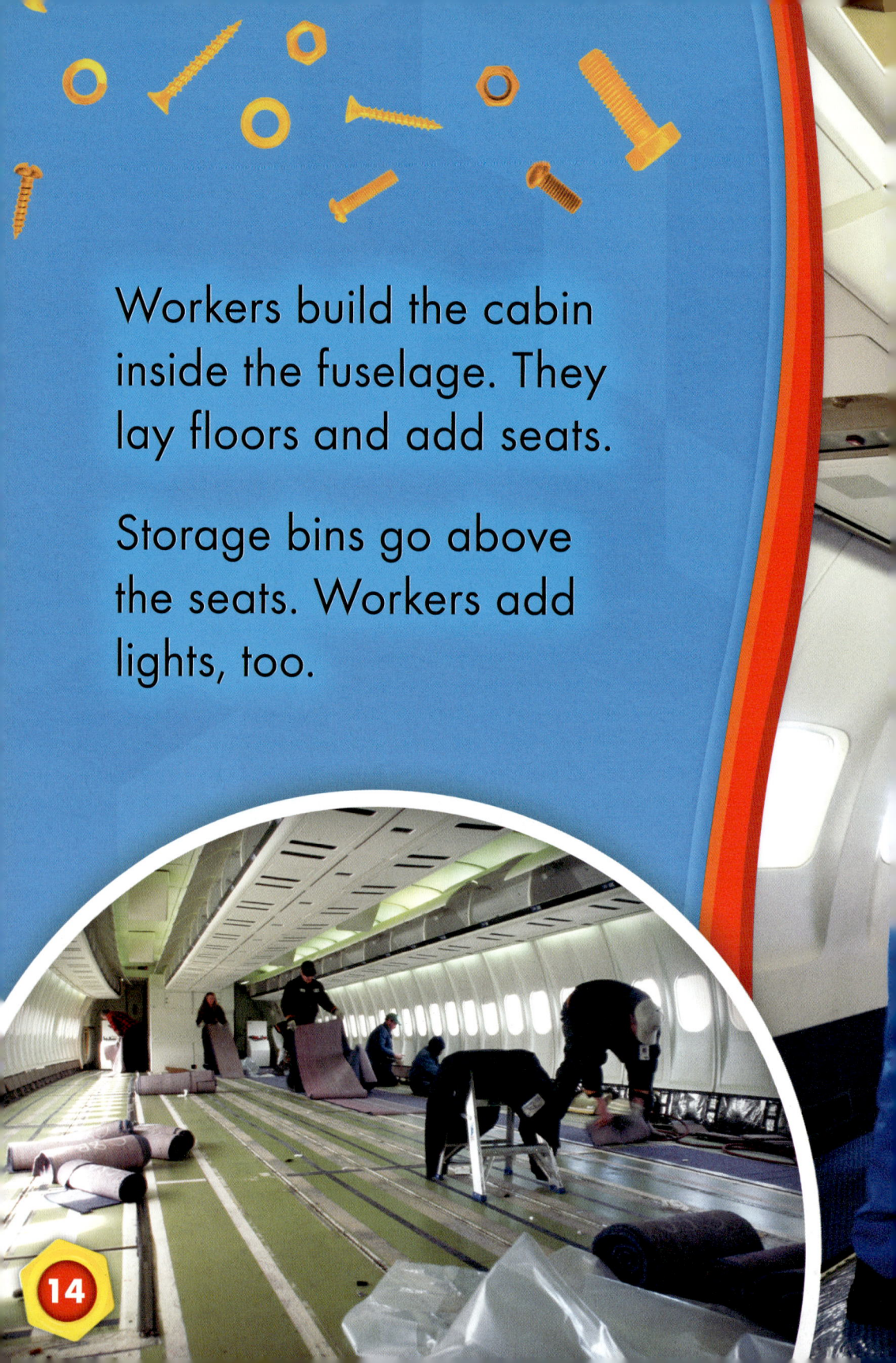

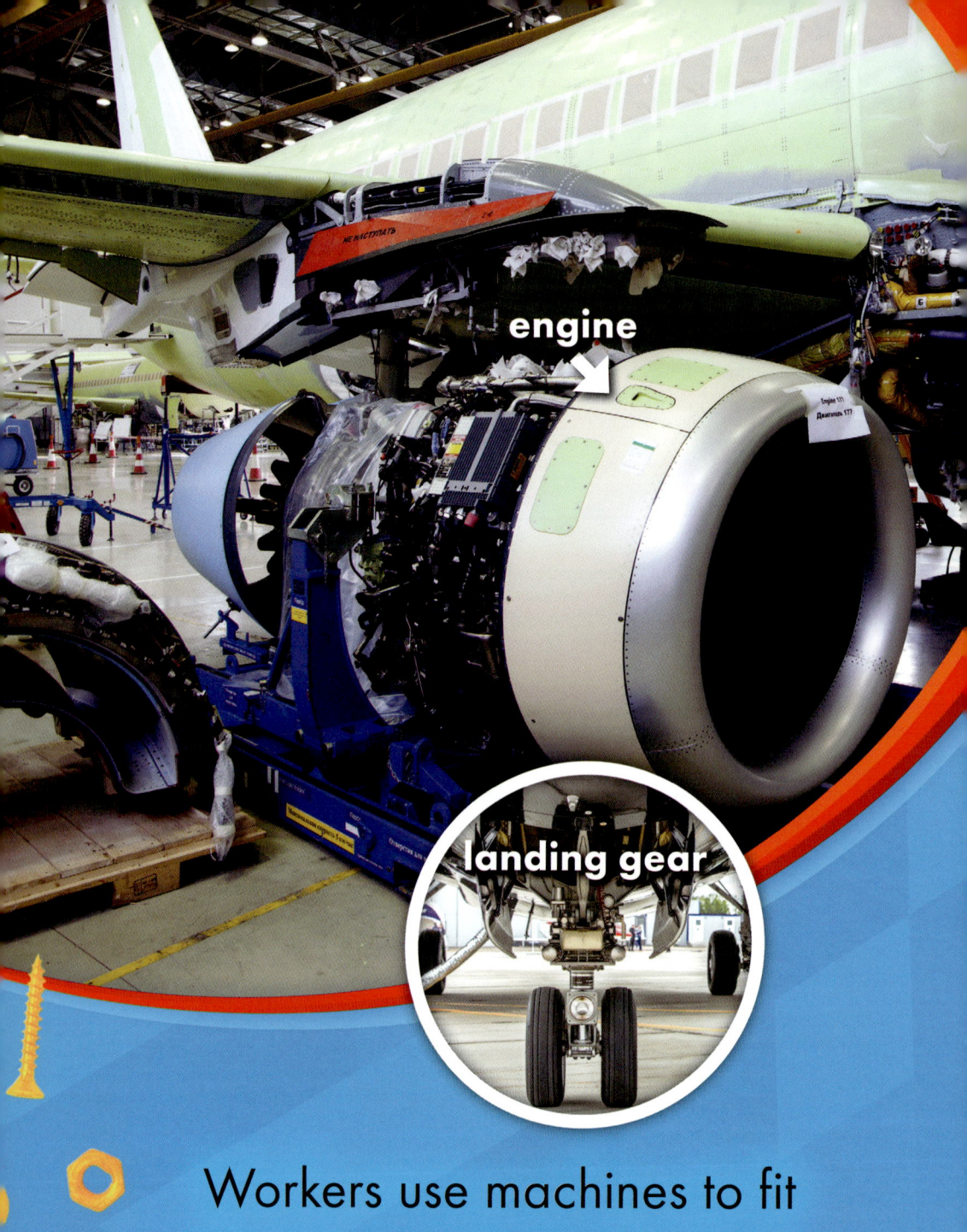

**engine**

**landing gear**

Workers use machines to fit the wings onto the fuselage. Engines go on the wings.

Workers connect landing gear to parts on the bottom of the fuselage.

## Roc Airplane

**Company**    Stratolaunch

**Year completed**    2019

**Length**    238 feet (72.5 meters)

**Wingspan**    385 feet (117 meters)

**Famous for**    the widest wingspan of any airplane

17

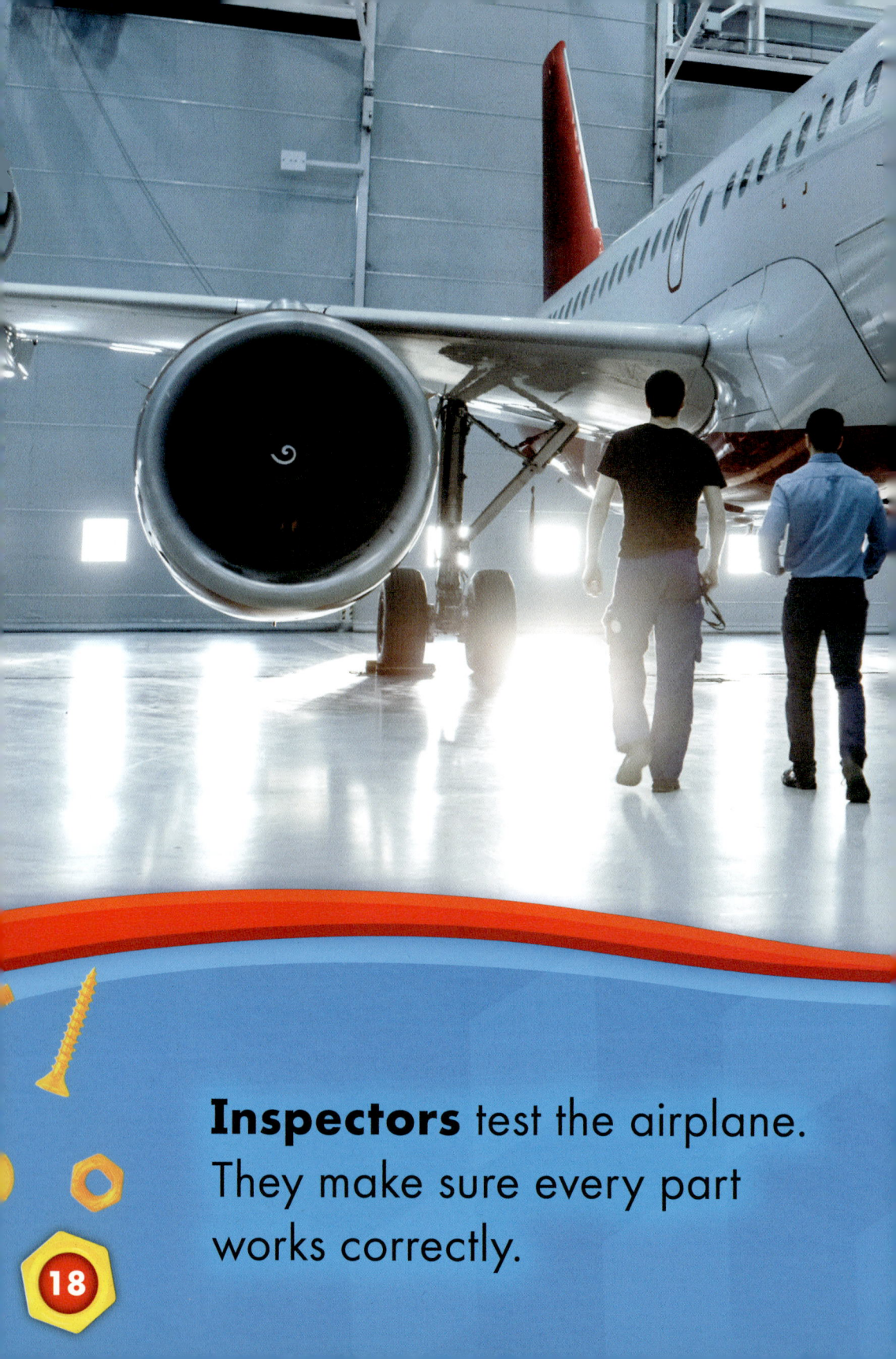

**Inspectors** test the airplane. They make sure every part works correctly.

18

# Step by Step

**1. Engineers make drawings and models.**

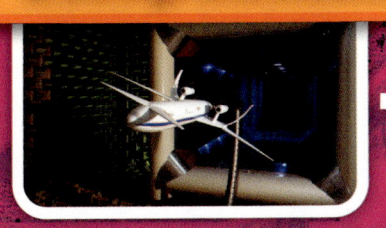

**2. Workers make the three-part fuselage.**

**3. Workers add a cockpit and the wings.**

**4. Workers finish the cabin.**

**5. Workers add engines and landing gear.**

**6. Inspectors do a safety check.**

The airplane has to be safe to fly.

# Up, Up, and Away!

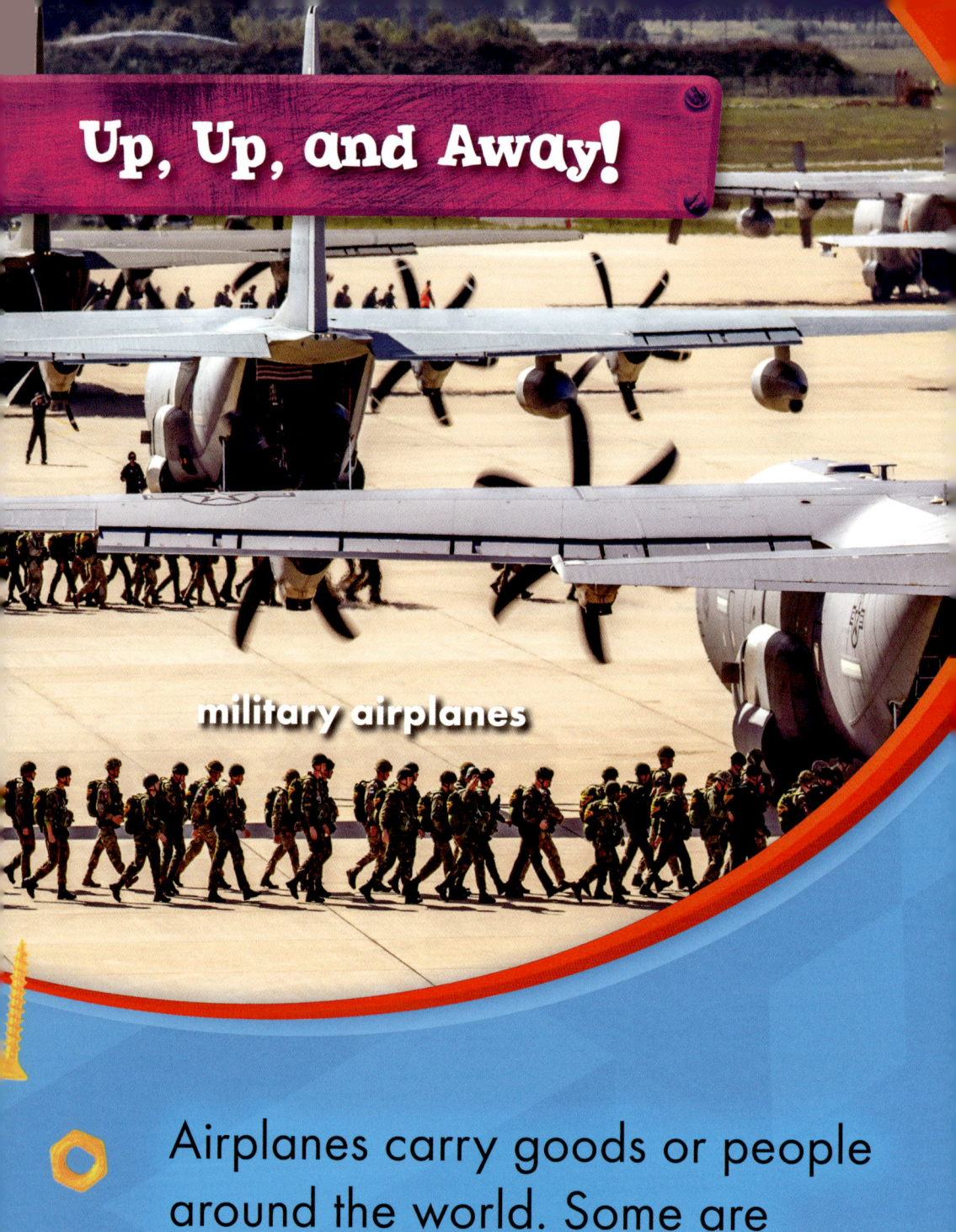

military airplanes

Airplanes carry goods or people around the world. Some are used by the **military**.

Many airplanes fly
for 30 years!

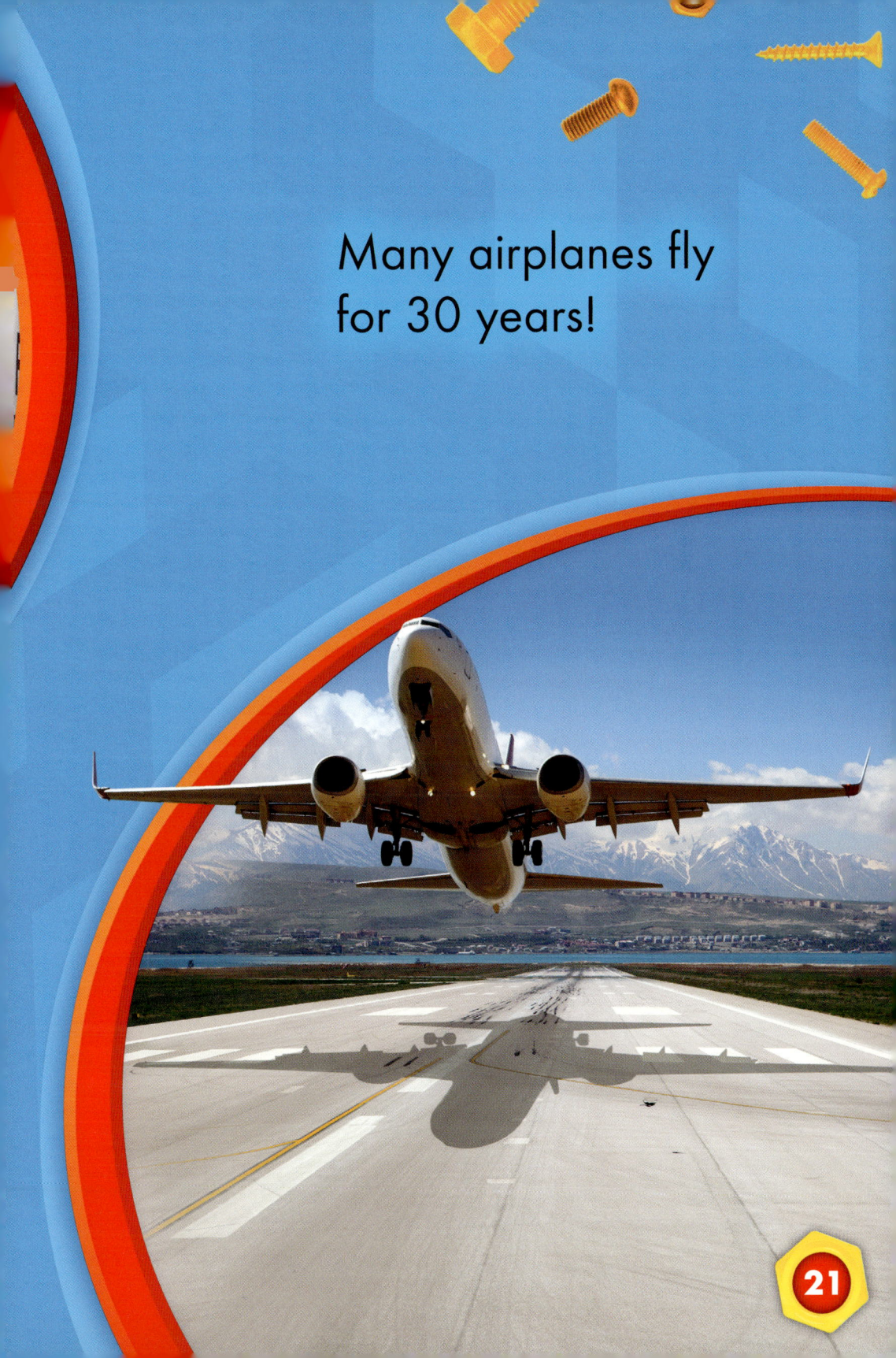

# Glossary

**aeronautical engineers**—people who are trained to design, build, and repair airplanes

**aluminum**—a strong, lightweight metal

**carbon fiber**—a strong, lightweight material made from woven pieces of carbon

**cockpit**—the part of an airplane where the pilot sits

**fuselage**—the main body of an airplane

**inspectors**—people who check to make sure work was done correctly

**insulate**—to fill with material that helps keep the air inside an airplane the right temperature

**military**—the armed forces

**models**—small versions of airplanes or other structures; models can be physical or digital.

**prototype**—the first full-size airplane from which other forms are made

**rivets**—metal bolts that are used to join two pieces together

**wind tunnels**—passages through which air is blown at specific speeds to test how air flows around an object

# To Learn More

## AT THE LIBRARY

Giulieri, Anne. *History of Flight*. North Mankato, Minn.: Capstone, 2021.

Lamichhane, Priyanka. *Planes*. Minneapolis, Minn.: Abdo Reference, 2024.

Young-Brown, Fiona. *The STEM of Airplanes*. New York, N.Y.: Cavendish Square Publishing, 2021.

## ON THE WEB

# FACTSURFER

Factsurfer.com gives you a safe, fun way to find more information.

1. Go to www.factsurfer.com.

2. Enter "airplane" into the search box and click $Q$.

3. Select your book cover to see a list of related content.

# Index

The images in this book are reproduced through the courtesy of: Skycolors, cover (top hero), pp. 16, 19 (step two); Juice Flair, cover (bottom hero), pp. 12, 14-15, 19 (step three); Synthetic Messiah, pp. 2-3; Friends Stock, p. 4; aappp, pp. 4-5, 19 (step five); Tomas Stevens/ Abaca/ Sipa USA/ AP Images, p. 6; Jozsef Soos/ Alamy, p. 7; Dino Fracchia/ Alamy, p. 8; vitals, p. 9 (carbon fiber); Richard Marx, p. 9 (rivets); Krysja, p. 9 (glue); fotosr52, p. 9 (aluminum); Leli, p. 9 (rubber); Sean Prior/ Alamy, p. 10; Daniel Reinhardt/ AP Images, p. 11; Sanit Fuangnakhon, p. 11 (cockpit); DenisProduction.com, p. 12 (aluminum frame); frank peters, p. 13 (airplane); Atosan, p. 13 (cabin); Tim Wright/ Getty Images, p. 14; Media_works, p. 16 (landing gear); Mario Tama/ Getty Images, p. 17 (Roc airplane); Gorodenkoff, pp. 18-19; Heinrich/ Alamy, p. 19 (step one); PhotopankPL, p. 19 (step four); industryviews, p. 19 (step six); VanderWolf Images, p. 20; muratart, pp. 21, 22-23, 24; Thierry Weber, p. 23.